KU-337-439

Once there was a
Raindrop

Schools Library and Information Services

S00000702999

For Rory - J.A

For Caiden, Lucy and Ben - M.G

DUDLEY PUBLIC LIBRARIES

L

702999 SCH

J546.22

First published in 2009 by Wayland
Copyright © Wayland 2009
This paperback edition published in 2012 by Wayland

Wayland, 338 Euston Road, London NW1 3BH

Wayland Australia
Level 17/207 Kent Street
Sydney NSW 2000

All rights reserved

Editor: Nicola Edwards
Designer: Paul Cherrill
Digital Colour: Carl Gordon

The right of Judith Anderson to be identified as the
author of the work has been asserted by her in
accordance with the Copyright, Designs and Patents
Act 1988.

British Library Cataloguing in Publication Data

Anderson, Judith, 1965-
Once there was a raindrop
1. Raindrops - Juvenile literature 2. Hydrologic cycle -
Juvenile literature
I. Title II. Gordon, Mike
551.5'77

ISBN: 978 0 7502 6735 9

Printed in China

Wayland is a division of Hachette Children's Books,
an Hachette UK company.
www.hachette.co.uk

Nature's Miracles

Once there was a
Raindrop

Written by
Judith Anderson

Illustrated by
Mike Gordon

WAYLAND

It's raining.
Rain is made up of lots
of tiny drops of water.

My teacher says each raindrop
is part of the water cycle.

When a raindrop falls to the ground it sinks into the earth and makes it wet and muddy.

Or it stays on the surface and forms puddles.

This water flows into drains and streams.

Or it collects underground.

The drains and streams
flow into lakes...

...and seas.

But that's not the end of the story. The sun warms the surface of the sea.

It's cold down here...!

The warmer water turns into water vapour, which rises into the air. This is called evaporation. You can't see water vapour, but it is all around us, in the air.

It's warm up here...!

That's how our wet
clothes get dry.

And that's where the water
in the birdbath has gone.

The water vapour rises high into the sky. As it gets higher, it cools down. The cool air turns the water vapour back into tiny droplets of water. These tiny droplets form clouds.

The same thing happens to the water vapour in your breath on a cold day!

19

The droplets of water
in the clouds get
bigger and heavier.

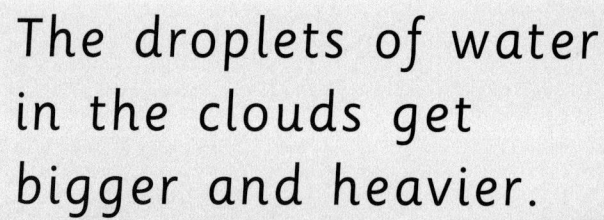

When they become too heavy to stay in the clouds, they fall as rain.

If the air is really cold,
the droplets freeze and
fall as snowflakes...

...or hailstones.

Sometimes
too much
rain falls.

24

Sometimes not
enough rain falls.

25

And sometimes
the rainfall is
just right.

Every drop of water on our planet
is recycled, over and over again.

That's why it is called
the water cycle!

NOTES FOR PARENTS AND TEACHERS

Suggestions for reading the book with children

As you read this book with children, you may find it helpful to stop and discuss what is happening page by page. Children might like to talk about the effect that the water is having on the landscape, people, animals and plants in many of the pictures. Page 25 shows what happens when not enough rain falls. Discuss the importance of water conservation with the children, and ask them if they know how to save water at home and at school.

The idea of a water cycle is developed throughout the book and is reinforced on pages 28-9 with the diagram drawn on the bathroom mirror. Ask the children why it is called a 'water cycle'. Can they think of any more cycles in nature? The other titles in the series may help them with this.

Children may be unfamiliar with some of the words in this book such as surface, water vapour, evaporation and recycled. Make a list of new words and discuss what they mean.

Nature's Miracles and the National Curriculum

The **Nature's Miracles** series satisfies a number of requirements of the Science curriculum at Key Stage 1. There are four titles about cycles in nature in the series: *Nature's Miracles: Once There Was a Raindrop*; *Once There Was a Caterpillar*; *Once There Was a Tadpole* and *Once There Was a Seed*. Each book encourages children to explore the natural world for themselves through direct observation and specific activities and emphasises developing a sense of responsibility towards plants, animals and natural resources.

Once There Was a Raindrop incorporates elements of both Geography and Science by helping young readers think about where water comes from and how it changes state through the processes of evaporation and condensation. The book also looks at the consequences of too much rain and too little rain on the environment.

Suggestions for follow-up activities

Evaporation can be a tricky concept for children because the water seems to 'disappear'. One way to show that water vapour is in the air is to ask children to blow onto a mirror or a window and observe the condensation that forms. Alternatively, observe how dew forms on grass and leaves or on top of cars overnight. Point out that when it is very cold, these droplets of water freeze and become frost.

Children can be helped to 'make' their own rain by placing a cold plate over a clear glass bowl of very hot water. (The plate can be made extra cold by placing a few ice cubes on top of it.) After a couple of minutes, droplets of water will have formed on the underside of the plate. Watch as the drops increase in size and start to drip back down into the bowl of water.

Can we predict how much rain will fall? Make a rain gauge by placing a plastic container on a flat, open outdoor site. Alternatively, use a plastic bottle with a funnel placed in the top to capture the water. This method prevents too much evaporation in hot weather. Children can use a ruler to measure the amount of rainfall at the same time each day over a period of a week or month and record their results on a chart. (Remember to empty the container after measuring each day.) Are the results as they expected?

31

Books to read

The Water Cycle by Sally Morgan (Wayland, 2011)
Cycles in Nature: The Water Cycle by Theresa Greenaway (Wayland, 2006)
The Drop Goes Plop by Sam Godwin and Simone Abel (Wayland, 1998)

Useful websites

http://kids.earth.nasa.gov/droplet.html
http://www.bbc.co.uk/schools/riversandcoasts/water_cycle/rivers/pg_02_flash.shtml

Index